Quit Chasing Squirrels... and Start Chasing Your Dreams

50 Hacks to Get You Started!

By Barb Hubbard

Copyright © 2023 Barb Hubbard

All rights reserved. No part of this book may be reproduced or used in any manner without the prior written permission of the copyright owner, except for the use of brief quotations in a book review.

To request permissions, contact the publisher at barb@barbhubbardcoaching.com.

ISBN: 979-8-9885246-0-1 (paperback)
ISBN: 979-8-9885246-1-8 (ebook)

First edition September 2023

Cover Design by Sydney Hubbard
Edited by Patricia White
Interior Edited and Designed by Danielle Anderson and the team at Ink Worthy Books

Disclaimer

The information in this book is based on the author's knowledge, experience and opinions. The methods described in this book are not intended to be a definitive set of instructions. You may discover other methods and materials to accomplish the same end result. Your results may differ.

By reading this document, the reader agrees that under no circumstances is the author responsible for any losses, direct or indirect, that are incurred as a result of the use of the information contained within this document, including, but not limited to, errors, omissions, or inaccuracies.

This book is not intended to give legal, financial, medical, or professional advice and is sold with the understanding that the author is not engaged in rendering legal, financial, medical, or other professional services or advice. If legal, medical, financial, or other expert assistance is required, the services of a competent professional should be sought to ensure you fully understand your obligations and risks.

Dedication

Dedicated to my children.

Always remember to chase your dreams.

Table of Contents

Introduction 1

Chapter 1: Your Passion Project is Waiting 11

Chapter 2: Why Can't I Get Started? 31

Chapter 3: Know Yourself 59

Chapter 4: Navigating the Hacks 85

Chapter 5: Accountability Hacks #1-8 97

Chapter 6: Energy Hacks #9-26 111

Chapter 7: Clarity Hacks #27-35 137

Chapter 8: Mindset Hacks #36-50 149

You've Reached the End! 171

50 Getting Started Hacks 175

Acknowledgements 179

About the Author 183

Introduction

This book is brought to you by Hacks #1, #3, #8, #10, #13, #18, #22, #33, #35, #40, #42, #43, and #45.

Let me tell you the ironic part of writing this book. I could not get started. I had the idea for this book for over a year before I actually sat down to write it. I procrastinated. I chased a lot of squirrels. I stopped and restarted many times. When you read the hacks presented here, let me assure you they've been tested. They work. Without them, you wouldn't be reading this!

I've also used these hacks to help hundreds of other people get started and restarted. For over 25 years, I've been working with kids and adults who have learning and attention issues. As an elementary school teacher and special educator, it was my job to work with children who had learning disabilities, autism, ADHD, etc. I helped them figure out how to get started with the work that they didn't want to do.

When I began working as a life coach for women who have ADHD, it was with pretty strong knowledge of how learning and attention issues affect productivity and progress, but I didn't yet realize the extent to which it can impact people's lives.

Unsurprisingly, I've since learned that nearly every one of my clients struggles to get started on some daily tasks. They avoid doing the little things such as the dishes or folding the laundry. What has surprised me is almost all have unfulfilled dreams of passion projects or side hustles. Their dreams may involve supporting a cause that's important to them, starting a small business to earn extra income, or writing a memoir.

Sadly, in most cases, they have placed these projects on the back burner because they struggle to get started and make progress. These are highly creative, talented, and ambitious individuals who have a lot to offer the world, and they are excited about their ideas, yet they've procrastinated for years.

When I realized so many dreams were being put aside, I started to pay attention. I had also mastered the art of procrastination and had seen it affect many others, but I wanted to understand why people put things off and figure out what to do about it to help them.

One of my clients is a fitness coach who supports older women. She had been working on a book, on and off, for several years. Life events and many distractions had gotten in her way. She often felt pressured to get her house in order and take care of daily tasks before she could focus on her book.

During our work together, she discovered strategies that worked well for her, and she began to write consistently.

Another client works in a male-dominated industry. She had been wanting to pass her state board exam for years, but distractions kept her from sitting down to study. The test date would sneak up on her, and she would panic. She knew that if she passed the exam, she could take on additional responsibility at her job. More importantly, she would be an even stronger role model for other women in a male-dominated workplace. Using the hacks in this book, this client began making progress toward her goal.

When I worked with kids, they became easily overwhelmed and were often reluctant to start on a project. These young students could be intensely interested in a topic, but they wouldn't pick up a book to do some research and learn more. Guess what? I discovered the same is true for adults! Being overwhelmed, distracted, and busy in life prevents too many people from getting started on the projects they are passionate about, meaningful pursuits that would have a positive effect on themselves and the lives of others. Since these projects are *important but not urgent*, they get pushed back.

Do you relate to these struggles? Do you have an idea for a project, but you haven't moved forward for months or years? Perhaps you have a proposal to submit, but you simply can't bring yourself to start typing. Maybe you have a fun side hustle and dream of quitting your day job, or you have a meaningful project you know would support hundreds of other people. Whatever it is you are putting off, now is the time to start! Big or little, delayed for a day or for years, you *can* start working on it and make it a reality.

I know, I know. This is the point when many people start to tune out. "Yeah... this sounds great, but it's not going to work for me."

Hear me out.

If you've had a project sitting on the sidelines for a while, you may have tried different approaches that simply don't work for you. They seem aimed at a completely different type of person who doesn't have your particular challenges, or the more common approaches you hear about feel misaligned with the way you work. I hear this all the time.

Rest assured that you are in the right place because this book is different.

This book is written with your individuality in mind. I'm not going to outline a ten-step approach to success that ends up making you feel as though you are broken. Your life doesn't fit inside a cookie cutter.

Instead, I'm going to help you uncover the strategies that work for *you*. I'll present 50 different hacks, so you can pick and choose the type of support you need in any given moment. This book will empower you to understand the magic of your unique brain and will provide you with options.

Now is the time to make your dreams a reality.

If ADHD is part of your story...

It's possible you have learning and attention issues—maybe even ADHD. Don't worry. I don't expect you to push through and overcome these challenges. I see you and all the issues that have been holding you back, and I have a deep understanding of how to help you move forward. I will offer ideas for you to try, so you can take the first step. When you figure out what works for your unique, neurodiverse brain, you will likely be propelled into action—your passion project is too important to stay on the back burner!

How to Use This Book

At this point, you are likely curious about how this book works. You may be thinking, *I don't have time*, which is a common way to avoid getting started. I know your life is busy, I know you have a tendency to chase squirrels, so I've created this book to be a handy, ongoing resource. You don't have to read it from cover to cover. You can pick and choose the parts that help support you. Lacking the time to read this book will not be the next excuse that prevents you from getting started.

In fact, I recommend reading only a couple of pages at a time and trying those hacks before continuing. Once you have found strategies that work, I've created space for you to mark those pages, so you can easily find them when you need them.

Most of these hacks are designed to help you in the moment, right when you are struggling to start a task. Some hacks provide a boost of energy, some help you organize your thoughts, and others challenge your thinking or help you create urgency around completing a task. Most can be done in fifteen minutes or less.

The first three chapters of this book dive into the reasons why you may be procrastinating and how to identify a starting point. These chapters also include journal prompts, so you can write down your thoughts. Chapter 4 explains the types of hacks and how to approach them. All the hacks are in Chapters 5–8.

Throughout the book, you'll find shaded sections that provide helpful tips and insights for readers who have, or suspect they have, ADHD. You will also find a helpful section in Chapter 3 called "Is ADHD Part of Your Story?"

Whatever your circumstances, you'll have 50 hacks to choose from to help you get started—or restarted. Kick your excuses to the curb and put an end to your procrastination.

Let's get started!

CHAPTER 1
Your Passion Project is Waiting

Have you ever been super excited about doing something you know will be amazing, fun, and impactful, and at the same time, you're also dreading it and avoiding it at all costs? It's like a confusing yin and yang, pulling you in both directions and effectively paralyzing you before you can make any move at all.

In fact, I felt this push and pull immediately before I sat down to write this chapter. As soon as I sat in my chair, I realized I needed to fill up my water bottle. I went downstairs to fill it, and halfway back up, in the middle of the staircase, I started a conversation with my teenager who was sitting in the kitchen. "I thought you were writing," they said. I responded, "I planned to, I want to, and I'm doing everything I can to avoid it. Why is it so *hard*?"

Don't get me wrong, I'm thrilled to write this book! I know it will impact so many people in a positive way. However, it feels overwhelming to put myself out there, and I dread the hours of sitting and writing, trying to avoid the squirrels. Also, I prefer immediate gratification, and that won't happen with such a big project. For all these reasons, I procrastinate.

Procrastination

Before we dive in, I want to distinguish between two different types of tasks people procrastinate on:

- Tasks they *do* want to do
- Tasks they *don't* want to do

I don't love doing the dishes. I mean, does anyone, really? I currently have a sink full of dirty dishes and will likely avoid them for the rest of the day. Getting the car's oil changed is another task I dislike. I will put it off until absolutely necessary. I procrastinate on these tasks because I don't want to do them. They are boring, tedious, and bothersome.

However, I love to write. Yet, it's the last task I do every week (if I do it at all). I procrastinate on writing because it requires more of my mental energy and because it can be overwhelming to tackle a big project with multiple steps. I want to write, and I enjoy it once I get going, but I have trouble getting started. My goal with this book is to help you stop procrastinating on this type of task, the one you really *want* to do but can't seem to start.

These two types of tasks can be characterized in a second way. The things we don't like doing often become *urgent* at some point. When you are out of clean underwear, you'll do the laundry! The urgency moves us into action. However, the things we like to do are often *important but not urgent*. We are passionate about these things. They are connected to our values and our purpose in life, but there's no urgency and no timeline, and they often don't make it into our daily schedule. It's easy to leave them on the back burner.

The hacks in this book will work for both types of procrastination, the tasks you *do* want to do and the ones you *don't*. But I want you to focus on the first type. The dishes and laundry will get done when it's urgent. Let's get you started on your dreams and goals, which are not urgent but are very important!

Squirrels, Willpower, and Dashed Hopes

You have incredible dreams. You're creative, resourceful, and care about others. There's a passion project that you *want* to start, but because it's not urgent, it never leaves the back burner. You've likely progressed through three phases of thought around this project. Let's see if you can recognize yourself in one or more of these stages.

In the first stage, you may not be sure how to find the time for your special project. At this point, it's only an idea, and you don't yet have a plan. Your day is likely spent reacting to whatever comes your way, and there is no time left for anything else. You pack the lunches, get the kids to school, sign the permission slips, hurry to work, answer the emails, work on the project that's due tomorrow, take a phone call, hurry home, make dinner, help the kids with homework, and crash into bed. Life is already busy, and adding one more thing may feel overwhelming.

You might also find you are easily sidetracked by all the squirrels. You answer a call. You spend too much time scrolling through social media. You check in with your family and do whatever they need you to do. It's hard to settle in and focus on your project with so many distractions in your life. As a result, your passions (and you) get pushed aside.

If ADHD is part of your story...

For people with ADHD, squirrels show up all day long. It's more than getting sidetracked; you may feel it's impossible to focus for any length of time. You may notice all the little movements, the almost undetectable sounds, and even different smells, and they pull you away from your task.

After you've had a bit of time to dream about your dream, you hit the second stage. You are determined. You commit to making time for your passion project. You tell yourself, "I'm going to sit and do this. I will find a place for it in my schedule, and I'm not going to do anything else until it's done."

During a coaching call a couple years ago, a client excitedly said, "I know what I have to do! I just have to be disciplined! *I just have to make myself do the work.*" She thought she had it figured out. She likely had observed others use this approach to get started and consistently work on projects. However, the following week, she reported it didn't work. Her "discipline" lasted about three days.

You too may have found this approach works for only a short time. Being "disciplined" drains our energy and leaves us looking at our project with feelings of overwhelm. The problem is that being disciplined is connected to willpower. Willpower ebbs and flows. In my observation, we have less of it when we are feeling overwhelmed or stressed, feelings that often come up when we are procrastinating. We can't count on willpower to be there when we need it.

If ADHD is part of your story...

The ADHD brain needs to be interested in the task. Using willpower alone is fruitless; you must create a sense of interest to get your brain's attention.

Then comes the last stage—the dashed hopes. Squirrels got in the way, the willpower didn't last, and you end up placing your dream on the back burner indefinitely. You are no longer merely procrastinating; you're giving up.

It's understandable! Why waste your thoughts on something that isn't ever going to happen? You may have a history of not living up to the expectations you or others have set. If you have learning or attention issues, you may genuinely feel as though you aren't capable of success (which isn't true, by the way).

But that idea—that dream—keeps nagging at you. You can't quite let it go.

You go up and down on a seesaw of fits and starts. You start, and life gets in the way. You begin again and then get distracted. You decide to push yourself and run out of energy. It doesn't feel good. You walk around with a lot of shame.

If ADHD is part of your story...

ADHD is more about regulating emotions than it is about regulating attention. People who struggle with ADHD frequently have strong emotions (anger, sadness, excitement), and those feelings can be overwhelming. If you have given up on your dream, take a look at the emotions behind it. Has the frustration subsided a bit at this point? When you think about how your project will impact others, does the excitement return?

Worse, you never move forward with that amazing, fun, and impactful dream. It sits there in the background.

You lose sight of the excitement because your brain is saying, "Who am I to do this anyway?"

At this point, you may be wondering if the problem is *getting started* or if it is *finishing*.

I often hear statements like, "I start things all the time! Teach me how to follow through—how to finish!"

If you can't seem to *finish* your passion project, let's take a look at finishing from a different perspective.

Finishing is REstarting.

It's starting over and over as many times as necessary until the project is complete. It's starting after you've been interrupted. It's starting after you've found yourself daydreaming. It's starting after you've put the project aside for a few weeks, months, or even years.

What if it could be easier to move from the first stage—having an idea—to the finish line?

What if there was a way to move forward with your passion project slowly, step by step, and consistently? What if there was a way to start and restart while always believing in yourself and knowing you'll be successful?

There is, and it starts with connecting or reconnecting with your passion. Let's set these dashed hopes aside and begin anew.

Connecting With Your Passion

Society would like us to believe the path to success is to set clear goals, be consistent, and work hard. A quick Google search reveals these messages:

- "With hard work and effort, you can achieve anything." ~ Antoine Griezmann

- "Winners embrace hard work. They love the discipline of it, the trade-off they're making to win. Losers, on the other hand, see it as a punishment. And that's the difference." ~ Lou Holtz

- "Success isn't always about greatness. It's about consistency. Consistent hard work leads to success. Greatness will come." ~ Dwayne Johnson

I think there's something missing here. I have yet to meet someone who can sit down each day and consistently focus on a dream. Life is too messy! These messages imply you simply need to work hard and be disciplined, which, in my observation, leads to dashed hopes. I don't believe hard work comes first. I think there is a step *before* hard work.

Passion needs to come first. When you tap into your passion, it will inspire you to do the hard work.

During my first conversation with a coaching client, I always ask, "Where do you want to be a year from now?" Without fail, I receive incredible answers. All the hopes and dreams come out. After all, most people who have ADHD or other learning or attention issues are also passionate and creative. They are driven with ambition to make a difference in the lives of others.

Here are some of the answers I've heard from clients:

- "I want to get through med school to become a doctor."

- "I want to create a preventative health curriculum for my university."

- "I want to write a book of poetry to encourage those who have been through trauma."

- "I want to start a business to support women who struggle with their menstrual cycle."

- "I want to create a blog to encourage stay-at-home moms."

- "I want to write a 'manifesto' for politicians."

- "I want to pass the state exam to move up in my career and be a role model for others."

- "I want to actively encourage others to vote."

In my first conversations with clients, we explore their dreams. Through my questions, they tap into their passion and bring all the positive emotions to the forefront. I ask for clarity around how their passions came up for them, who those passions might support, and what the impact of those passions will be when they reach their goals. In less than an hour, they are excited and ready to start the hard work.

One of my clients shared that she had about five business ideas she was pursuing. She was excited about all of them but making little progress on any. She lacked consistency, she constantly jumped from one idea to the next, and her self-diagnosed ADHD was keeping her from being focused. She was looking to develop a game plan, as well as create some structure and accountability in her hectic day.

Through some discussion, we identified the project she was most excited about and that would have the most immediate impact. She dreamed of growing this business, and we tapped into her passion during our conversation. Fast forward six months, and this client now has a day job that she loves, *and* she is growing a side hustle at the same time!

Another client and I began working together toward the beginning of the pandemic. She reached out looking for more routine in her day and wanted to develop healthier habits.

Through our initial conversation, I discovered she was also extremely passionate about helping stay-at-home moms. She had started to create a website and blog, but daily life events left her with little time. She tried to force herself to sit down and work on it with little success.

After some conversations around the women she would impact with her blog, she found renewed passion. She was able to find time to write here and there, and she found she didn't need to force herself to write or create the perfect schedule to get started.

Connecting with your passion is key. Through conversations, my clients share their ideas, reconnect with their hopes and dreams, and are then ready to get to work. It happens almost as if by magic!

Yes, work is needed, but when the strong, positive emotions are at the top of your mind, it's much easier to get started.

If ADHD is part of your story...

One of the strengths of ADHD is passion. Don't overlook your creative mind, endless ideas, and compassion for others. Use these strengths to your advantage.

What do these examples and stories inspire in you? Think about your passions and, if you already have one, your project. Visualize yourself doing these things. See it happening. Talk with a friend about it to get clarity around your ideas and to increase your excitement.

Please don't think your passion project has to impact many people. It might be something extremely personal to you. Here are some other ideas to prompt your thinking:

- Successfully launch a business to be a role model for your child.

- Clean out a storage space to create room for a new chapter of life.

- Earn enough money in a side hustle to pay for your child's college costs.

- Travel with a loved one.

- Take a mission trip.

- As a solopreneur, have flexibility to work from anywhere and work fewer hours.

Making an impact can start with a tiny step. The first step in getting started (or restarted) is to identify with your passion. Even if it's not yet a specific project, think about what lights you up. Visualize it. Write it down. Tell others about it. This will ignite the energy you need to identify your project and get started.

Feel that energy? I'm excited for you, and I don't even know what you're thinking! Take that energy and use it. Your dreams are valid. You can do this. Simply take the first step.

Life is always going to get in the way. A week won't go by when something doesn't pop up and pull you off task. There will always be more to do than you have time for, but the reality is your life will be happier, and you will experience more fulfillment if you start working toward your dreams.

If you get sidetracked, don't worry. Reconnect with your passion and restart.

The time is now. Take the first step.

Journal Prompts (5–10 minutes)

Say what? I'm giving you homework? Yes! Pausing and taking a few moments to write down your thoughts will make it more likely for you to actually start on your passion project. You'll find more journal questions to consider at the end of Chapters 2 and 3. If you need additional space for your thoughts, feel free to pull out a separate piece of paper or notebook.

1. Write down what you are passionate about. What do you love? Who do you love to support? What brings you joy?

2. If you haven't already, choose an idea. If time and money were not factors, what would you create? Who would you help or support? Write down a few ideas.

3. If you've started on a project, think about the underlying reasons why you began. Reconnect with the joy this dream ignites. Who does it impact? What will you feel when it is out in the world?

CHAPTER 2
Why Can't I Get Started?

I'm guessing you might be thinking it's simply *not* that easy to get started. You are concerned the excitement and energy from thinking about your passion project won't last. There are too many things that can get in the way.

I know you probably have a history of struggling to get started. I also know you've likely started several times and then stopped. Like me, you might have a tendency to chase squirrels! Before you feel pressured to take action or take a leap without a parachute, let's talk about why you've struggled in the past and what to do about it.

Several years ago, a client shared that she would wake up in the morning excited about the day ahead and jump out of bed with enthusiasm, but by the time she would sit down at her desk, all motivation would be gone. She'd sit and stare at her computer, and nothing would get done.

She was the first of many clients who shared a similar concern. "If I could only get started," became a phrase I heard nearly every week. Sometimes, it was about the laundry or another household task. More often than not, these people could not get started on something important to them, something that, hours earlier, they were excited to do.

We had conversations about their dreams and passion projects. They knew they could make an impact on their own lives and on the world, and they had the initial excitement to begin. The projects were brought to the forefront and added to the schedule, but the moment would come to spend time on it, and all motivation would be lost. There was more going on than simply the need to tap into their positive emotions around the project.

In response, I started compiling a list of "Getting Started Hacks" (which eventually became this book). I had many ideas and tricks to try, but it quickly became evident that clients were more successful if I helped them identify their *why* first—why they couldn't get started in the first place.

Sure, these hacks have been designed so that you can flip to the back of the book and try the first one you come across. You might even land on one that works for you on your first try. However, in my experience, your success is more likely if you put some thought into the reason(s) you can't get started. Knowing why will point you in the right direction to get the help you need, so let's spend some time talking about that.

For example, are you struggling to find time for your passion project? If your schedule is full, you might not think you have enough time or energy to start something new. You may need to find a hack that fills up your drained battery.

Are you easily distracted? You might need to consider working in a different location in order to remain focused. Or perhaps you need someone who will check in on your progress.

Do you feel as though the project is too big? Are you having trouble knowing where to start? Perhaps you are nervous about needing to learn something new. If you are feeling overwhelmed, there are hacks for you.

It's extremely helpful if you can narrow down the immediate reason you can't get started. The client from my previous example shared that she had so many thoughts in her head and so many possible tasks to complete that she struggled to figure out where to start. She was at the very first steps of launching a health coaching business, which involved coaching calls, taking notes, creating meal plans, writing blogs, scheduling appointments, and so much more. She wanted her work to be perfect in order to please the limited number of clients she had, and there were many new business tasks to learn.

After we identified the specific reasons she couldn't get started, I shared hacks to help her clarify her thoughts prior to making the calls.

When she had a plan for the day (Hack #28), and she took the time to visualize the first task (Hack #30), she was able to get started without as much hesitation. We also worked on lessening the need for perfection (Hack #36). Armed with these hacks, she stopped procrastinating and started! Her experience illustrates that if you understand *why* you are struggling, you are more likely to choose a hack (or hacks) that will work.

After a couple years of suggesting various hacks to my clients and exploring why they were struggling to get started, I began to notice a pattern. There are some common reasons we can't, won't, or simply don't get started. Sometimes it's one reason, and sometimes they overlap in a tangled web, but it generally comes down to these five reasons:

1. We are too busy.

2. We are distracted.

3. We are overwhelmed.

4. We have no motivation.

5. We have followed the wrong advice.

Busy-ness

Our society hails busy as a badge of honor, and it's not.

I'm not sure when we began praising busy people. I'm dating myself, but I feel as though when I was growing up, my friends and family spent more time sitting and relaxing. We didn't have kids' activities every night and every weekend, all year long. My parents didn't work in the evenings or on the weekends.

With the internet and cell phones, especially smartphones, we can now be reached anywhere at any time. It's common to "work" at all hours, 24/7. We are always accessible, and, therefore, always busy.

Busy people receive a lot of praise—praise for being on that extra committee, praise for volunteering extra hours, praise for driving kids around, or praise for working extra hours to get the project done.

Praise is addictive. We love compliments and thrive on appreciation, so we add more to our lives.

The opposite also happens. When we have "downtime," we aren't sure what to do with ourselves. We feel kind of odd sitting around, as though something is a little off and it's not really okay, so we add more to our lives.

On and on it goes until we fill up our schedules with so much stuff that we truly don't have time or energy for the ideas and projects that make up our dreams... Or so we think.

The truth is we could probably ditch a few (maybe many) of the activities on our calendar, but it will take some effort and some tough conversations to off-load some of those commitments.

I encourage you to go back to your passions (Chapter 1). The energy you felt at that time will make the decisions and conversations easier. If you feel too busy to get started, it's time to reevaluate your priorities.

Even after you make your passion project a priority and find time in your busy schedule, it can be hard to find the energy to get started. If this is the case for you, choosing a hack that boosts your energy (Chapter 6) may be the trick.

Distraction

You have your project in mind. You are excited about it. You are ready to get started. Then, your attention is diverted... *squirrel!* You can't seem to stay on task.

I have identified two types of distractions:

1. Little bits of sensory stimuli that interrupt your thoughts
2. Requests from others in your life

Let's talk about the sounds, smells, and sights:

- The "ding" of a text notification
- The doorbell next door
- The dog snoring
- The ice falling in the freezer
- The smell of your roommate's lunch
- Your coworker's perfume
- The breeze blowing paper around
- The bird flying by the window
- Your stomach grumbling

> ### *If ADHD is part of your story...*
>
> *You might be extra sensitive to the tiny sounds, scents, and sights. Be aware of what distracts you and set yourself up for success by choosing a work location that avoids these. Many people find it helpful to work in a setting with background noise—a coffee shop, for example—or by listening to music or the TV.*

So many distractions!

The problem isn't the sound, smell, or sight itself. It's your response to it. Do you let it pull you off task into a daydream, do you get up and walk away from your work, or do you set up your environment for success? Do you chastise yourself when you've spent ten minutes off task, or do you notice you are inattentive and purposefully get back to work?

Distractions only derail you if you let them.

The truth is, we do have quite a bit of control over our environment and the distractions that derail us. We can turn off notifications. I promise it's okay for someone to wait a bit before hearing back from you. We can sit in a less distracting environment. We can choose to ignore the sights and sounds around us.

Attention works like a muscle. You can strengthen it by starting small and focusing for short periods of time. By creating a supportive environment that is distraction free, you can learn to sustain focus for longer and longer periods. Don't beat yourself up if you get pulled off task. Instead, notice what caused it and purposefully refocus your thoughts.

In addition to the environmental stimuli, let's consider the interruptions you face throughout the day. Think of the people in your life—kids, spouse, boyfriend, best friend, colleagues, boss, parent. Think about how often you do something for one of them. What percentage of your day is spent completing tasks for others?

In and of itself, doing stuff for others is not a bad thing, but it may turn into "people pleasing," a harmful behavior, when it's at the expense of our own needs. When we stop doing things for ourselves (exercising, eating healthy, sleeping, showering) or consistently choose to complete tasks for others before working on our own goals and dreams, it becomes time to stop and look at how it is impacting our health and our schedule.

People pleasing overlaps with busy-ness. Often, when we are busy, we begin reacting to whatever comes our way each day, chasing squirrels, instead of intentionally completing tasks. An email notification pops up, and we click on it to respond. Our child tells us they have a project due the next day, and we jump in to help get it done. Our boss calls after hours, and we stop what we're doing to answer.

While we'll probably never completely stop the onslaught of requests we receive, we are in control of our responses, and we *can* say no or delay our response. If your passion project is your priority, you *can* carve out time to work on it. It is not selfish to make time for your own goals. In fact, since your dreams will likely help others, I'd bet it's the opposite of selfishness!

If distractions are a reason you are not getting started, you'll need to choose a hack that will help you avoid them.

Overwhelm

Along with being busy and feeling distracted comes the feeling of being overwhelmed. We have an excessive number of things to do, but there's also the overwhelm that comes when a project is too big or too scary.

The client I shared about in Chapter 1 was overwhelmed with both a busy, distracted life and the prospect of needing to learn a ton of new skills.

During our first call, she described several different projects she was excited about. She was trying to do them all plus work a full-time job! The demands on her time were overwhelming. Despite her passion around creating a new business, she wasn't sure where to start.

She had decision fatigue. She had thought through all her options, but there were too many of them. Going over and over the choices and trying to act on every one of them left her feeling exhausted. This, in addition to being quite busy, kept her from making any decision at all.

If ADHD is part of your story...

For people who have learning and attention issues, we might call this ADHD paralysis. If you have ADHD, decisions can be overwhelming. You have hundreds of ideas (because you are a creative and divergent thinker) and no idea where to begin. You might spend all of your time researching or talking to others about your project without making much progress, or, as was the case with my client, you freeze and don't move forward on anything.

My client was most passionate about one particular side hustle, but she wasn't moving forward with it because there was so much to do that she didn't know where to start. In addition to her full schedule, her project had an overwhelming number of steps and a huge learning curve. Teaching yourself how to do new tasks can be quite scary! Together, we discussed each step, and she took it a day at a time. Learning only one new skill or handling only one hurdle was doable, and her feelings of being overwhelmed soon lessened.

If feeling overwhelmed is the reason you aren't getting started, there are quite a few hacks for you to try.

Lack of Motivation

Much of what we accomplish each day happens because we feel motivated to do it. Positive or negative, the feeling of excitement or urgency offers the incentive to start a task. However, you can't count on feeling motivated all the time, and waiting for this elusive feeling may be yet another reason why you can't get started.

If you consider what you do accomplish each day, my guess is you'll find you had incentives or strong reasons for completing those tasks. Much of what we get done brings results that feel good: a thank you, a "like," money, kind words. We feel good when we look around at a clean kitchen or when we've done something kind for someone else. Also, our brains respond favorably to meeting deadlines and crossing items off our to do list.

Do you see what all of these examples have in common? Most provide instant gratification, an immediate sense of accomplishment. Our brains love this! It's harder to find motivation when we don't anticipate getting a reward right away. For example, as I write this book, no one praises me when I finish a chapter, and the book won't be completely finished for months. That's why it's hard to sit down to work for an hour or two on this long-term project!

> ### *If ADHD is part of your story...*
>
> *Everyone likes immediate gratification. However, if you have ADHD, your brain has an even harder time getting started on a task if the finish line is too far away. Your brain needs more frequent praise, rewards, competition, or immediate results because it struggles with a sense of time. For this reason (and others), long-term projects such as your passion project are tricky to start. When the end zone is so far away, it's hard to find motivation.*

Remember, it's easier to act on tasks that feel urgent—the sink full of dirty dishes, the request from a loved one, etc. Our passion projects are often *important but not urgent*. If we've spent years reacting only to urgent daily tasks, we may not know how to live any other way.

I had a client who worked in a fast-paced career filled with nearly constant calls, emails, and requests. She thrived in this setting. She loved her job. However, she also had to write detailed, lengthy reports, and she struggled to get started on these. We tried a lot of hacks, mostly those that would give her a quick boost of motivation for the time she had set aside for this work.

While the hacks often worked in the short term, she continued to lack motivation from week to week. It was not until we addressed her mindset for sitting down to write (Hack #39) and created some healthy habits (Hacks #23 and #25) that she was able to get started with less struggle. She needed to find ways to keep an ongoing feeling of motivation for the different aspects of her career.

Motivation is not only about the impulse or catalyst to get started on a task—the urgent push—but it's also about your overall desire and interest in the project. That is why I asked you to tap into your passion in Chapter 1. You need passion and excitement for *sustained* motivation. In addition, your health, your happiness, and your mindset affect your motivation. You may need to address these areas, so you don't rely too much on quick motivation boosts.

My clients often tell me they "only need a little motivation." They *want* the answer to be a quick fix because it seems easier than changing their daily habits. The problem is that motivation is much like willpower or discipline; it doesn't always last. You can create bursts of energy, but those bursts are only short-term solutions. Relying solely on quick motivation boosts will eventually drain your energy. You also need to work on your healthy habits and mindset to create an inner, longer lasting incentive for getting started on your passion project. There are hacks for that!

The Wrong Advice

If you've had an idea for a passion project for a while, you may have picked up a book or watched a video to help you get started. Many well-meaning people publish books, speak at conferences, and share their prescriptions for success.

They say things such as, "Follow this morning routine for a productive day," or, "These four rules are the key to your success!"

These people are often charismatic, encouraging, and offer hope, so you probably tried their ideas. Adding in the possibility that these ideas worked well for a friend or colleague, and you were hooked. You thought you had found the answer to getting started!

If you were lucky, you had mixed results. Perhaps you pulled out a few helpful strategies and were able to move forward with that. However, people tell me far too often that they ended up with a sense of defeat. They tried. It didn't work. They felt as though something was wrong with them, and they gave up.

It's not that others don't have good ideas, and it's not that they are necessarily wrong. Their strategies do work for many people. The problem is that it may be the wrong advice for *you*. They seem to suggest that their approach will work for everyone, but I've discovered, through my own experiences and my work with clients, that some ideas don't work well for the neurodivergent community, and that may have been one of the reasons your hopes were dashed.

You may have heard of a productivity strategy called "Eat the Frog." This was made popular a few years back by Brian Tracy, and it works well for a lot of people. It involves choosing the hardest task—the one you've been avoiding—and doing it first. When you've accomplished the most difficult item on your to-do list, everything else seems easy, and you have a productive day. When this idea first became popular, I tried it... and it didn't work for me. I could not (and still can't) do the hardest task first.

Through some trial and error, I figured out how to tackle the difficult tasks, but I first had to come to terms with the fact that my brain didn't work like so many others.

Being let down by the wrong advice often brings shame and frustration. Trying several different ideas without success is bound to make you feel drained and depleted. Why in the world would you think you are capable of reaching your goals if none of these expert strategies work for you? Something must be wrong with you, right?

Wrong! In contrast (and in reality), I believe there is more than one path to achieving your dreams. I am in favor of figuring out what works for you through a bit of reflection, trial, and error and creating *your own* rules and prescriptions. Take one or two ideas from different experts, throw in a few of your own ideas, and put them all together to fit your unique brain. *That's* the key to productivity and success!

If you've fallen into the trap of reading all the books and trying all the apps, and you still haven't found what works, you are not alone, and it might be one of the reasons you aren't able to get started.

Consider the strategies in this book. Take what works for you and leave what doesn't. Know that you are not broken. The fact that other advice didn't work for you has no impact on what you can achieve!

Restarting

All the same reasons apply to those who haven't found the finish line for their dreams. You became too busy, and life got in the way for a while. You stopped working because your child needed help with homework. You walked away from the project because you couldn't figure out the next step to take. The experts were no help, and you lost all motivation.

Perhaps you also found yourself feeling increasingly frustrated at your lack of progress. In addition to all the very real reasons why you couldn't restart—busy-ness, distractions, overwhelm—you also felt as though you were trying all the strategies, and none of them worked for *you*.

When it comes to trying strategies, you need to know yourself and what works for you. In the next chapter, we will explore this idea, so you can narrow down the hacks that might work best for you.

Whether you are taking the very first step, or you're on your tenth *re*start, your procrastination does not make you a failure. Your passion project is waiting. The time is now.

Journal Prompts (5–15 minutes)

Remember, pausing for a few moments and writing down your thoughts will make it more likely for you to actually get started. If you have learning and attention issues, it's likely you have a ton of thoughts. You are creative and have a lot of ideas, but you also need to slow down and sort through those thoughts to pinpoint the reasons why you can't get started. Consider these questions and pull out an additional piece of paper or notebook if you need more space.

1. Take a few minutes to consider what may be holding you back. Check off the areas that apply and write down your thoughts about each one.

    ____ busy-ness   ____ distraction

    ____ overwhelm   ____ no motivation

    ____ wrong advice

Thoughts:

Additional questions to prompt your thoughts (if needed):

2. What is a small change you could make this week to adjust your schedule or work location in order to reduce your commitments or distractions?

3. Does your project seem too big? What is the tiniest first step you can take to get started (making a phone call, writing a paragraph, creating an outline)?

4. What tasks do you accomplish during a regular week? What motivates you to do them?

5. Think about the books you've read, the videos you've watched, and the advice you've been given. What is one takeaway that does work for you?

CHAPTER 3

Know Yourself

You've reignited your passion, you've explored the reasons you haven't been able to get started, and you may feel ready to begin now. I know you are excited, so feel free to jump ahead and try one or more of the hacks in the second half of this book. You might land on one that works well for you. You can always circle back to read the rest of the book later. There's not only one right way to read this book, and you don't have to read it cover to cover. Do what works for you!

If you aren't quite ready, or if you'd like to narrow it down a bit further, continue reading this chapter. Taking the time to learn how your brain works and identify your preferences will bring more clarity and help guide you to the most effective hacks for you.

If ADHD is part of your story...

The ADHD brain is impulsive. You might find that it's hard to hold yourself back from trying a hack or two right now. Go ahead! However, be aware there is a whole chapter of goodness right here that you may find useful at a later date.

Your Unique Path

One of the biggest reasons people abandon their dreams is because they have tried to achieve their goals by following someone else's path to success. In addition to leading busy, distracting lives, they have often placed their dreams on the back burner after attempts to follow someone else's footsteps have failed.

In today's world, we are surrounded by information and ideas. On a daily basis, we receive tips from influencers and experts. When we observe someone else's success, it's easy to jump to the conclusion that their ideas should work for everyone. But, if what they suggested didn't work for you, it's probably because they didn't know your unique needs; it's not because there is anything wrong with you.

Consider that when a chef creates a delicious new dish, they add ingredients and spices they feel most people will enjoy. They know what their friends, family, and customers will enjoy because they've spent time with them and observed their likes and dislikes. They offer the new dish to their customers, and the majority of them love it! It doesn't mean everyone will love it. It doesn't even mean everyone will even like it. If I dislike the new dish, is there something wrong with me? No!

The same is true for self-help and productivity authors, speakers, and experts. They are writing to their audience. If what they suggest doesn't work for you, don't blame yourself. You are unique. They don't know you.

Let's take it a step further. You meet the chef and share what *you* like to eat. Perhaps they even introduce you to a few new foods, and as you try them, you give feedback about what you like and dislike. The chef then creates a brand new dish for you, and you love it.

Figuring out how to get started is as personal as creating the perfect culinary treat. You have to take into consideration what works for you and what doesn't, without judging yourself along the way. Just as you don't criticize yourself for not liking olives, you don't need to beat yourself up if you prefer to work late at night, even though the experts say early morning is when most people are more productive.

If you have learning and attention issues, your brain is wired differently, and there's nothing wrong with it—far from it—but it may present you with unique challenges that need unique solutions and a unique path forward. Most of the self-help and productivity books out there were *not* written with your distinctive brain in mind, but with a little guidance, you can uncover what works.

If ADHD is part of your story...

People with ADHD have many strengths to pull from—resilience, creativity, perseverance, intuition, imagination, and observation. You are more than capable of finding a new path forward!

When I was teaching, students came to my classroom for a couple hours each day to learn to read, write, or complete math problems. They came to see me because they had been identified as needing individualized approaches to learning those skills. One of my goals was to help my students understand themselves. I wanted them to identify their strengths and to look at their weaknesses with curiosity as they figured out personalized solutions. I worked with them in small groups using methods their general education teachers did not use. I got to know them. Together, we learned what worked and what didn't, and they progressed in all academic areas.

Coaching is similar. People reach out to work with me so they can be more productive and focused. They have specific projects, and they need personalized solutions to get started and stay on track. We talk about their likes, dislikes, and personalities, and we determine a customized path forward.

Now it's your turn to be your own coach! Know yourself and be yourself to get started on that passion project!

Personality Frameworks

Personality frameworks are a great way to learn more about yourself as you figure out what strategies you need to have in place in order to quit chasing squirrels. I love personality frameworks! I take the quizzes and reflect every chance I get. I learn a bit more about myself every time, and I have a new understanding of how I can be more effective at completing things. Each one is a bit different and offers a unique insight into the personality.

Here are a few of the most popular[1]:

1. Myers-Briggs Type Indicator – This assessment helps identify how people perceive the world around them as they make decisions in their everyday lives. It explores four categories: introvert/extrovert, sensing/intuition, thinking/feeling, and judging/perceiving. Knowing your "type" can give you insights into how to best communicate with others and increase your productivity.

2. Enneagram – This personality test places you in one of nine categories. It can help you

---

[1] Myers-Briggs Type Indicator www.myersbriggs.org
Enneagram www.enneagraminstitute.com
Clifton Strengths www.gallup.com

understand your fears, what motivates you, and, in turn, offer a greater understanding of yourself.

3. CliftonStrengths – This framework identifies your strengths and talents as they relate to working with others in the workplace or on teams. It looks at 34 characteristics and offers each person a unique ranking, allowing them to uncover what they naturally do best.

Here are a couple of my personal favorites, though maybe lesser known[2]:

1. The Four Tendencies by Gretchen Rubin – This framework identifies how you respond to outer and inner expectations (a goal someone else expects of you versus a personal goal) and provides specific strategies on how to get stuff done.

---

[2] The Four Tendencies https://gretchenrubin.com/quiz/the-four-tendencies-quiz/
 Via Character Strengths www.viacharacter.org

2. Via Character Strengths – This inventory of strengths provides you with your top positive personality traits. Of 24 traits, a few examples are curiosity, gratitude, kindness, bravery, and perseverance. Using your top strengths provides greater engagement, motivation, and happiness.

One of my very first coaching clients was struggling to get started in the mornings. She was a consultant who loved supporting women in improving their health. Her role was in line with her passion, and her dream was to improve the lives of many by sharing healthy household products. However, she had to make a lot of phone calls—often cold calls—which she didn't love.

Through the Via Character Strengths quiz, we discovered her top strength was creativity. I thought she could use this strength to create beautiful flyers or displays. However, she took a different approach that ultimately changed her daily routine forever.

She loved to sew, paint, and do crafts, so she allowed herself 20 minutes each morning to dive into one of her creative projects. After this short amount of time, she felt great, thus energizing her to make her calls. Tapping into her creativity boosted her energy and confidence. The crafts she worked on didn't even have anything to do with her business!

Much can be learned through personality assessments. If you discover you are more of an introvert, you can structure your day so you have time to recharge after a luncheon or large meeting. If you realize you are a night owl, you can release the judgment around not accomplishing as much in the mornings.

Knowing your strengths will boost your confidence and, in turn, provide the energy needed to start on some harder tasks.

I encourage you to explore these or other frameworks as you get to know yourself and create a customized path for success.

Self-Discovery

Another simple and powerful way to get to know yourself is to do a bit of self-discovery. Rather than taking an assessment someone else created, self-discovery is more freely flowing. Through reading, journaling, meditation, or conversation with a friend (or coach), simply think about yourself.

What do you like about yourself? What would you like to change? What strategies work well for your motivation and productivity?

Be curious. Put some thought into your answers. You may have some preconceived notions about what is "right" or what is "best." That could be exactly what is holding you back from getting started.

When you look at the truth with curiosity and let go of the shame, you will be more likely to accept what truly works for you. Remember, you are unique!

> ### *If ADHD is part of your story...*
>
> *For people with learning and attention issues, you likely have known since you were little that traditional strategies don't always work for you. You may have spent much of your life trying to fit in and force the strategies to work. This has likely created a lot of frustration and shame. When you've always wanted to fit in and be like everyone else, it might be counterintuitive for me to suggest that you need to embrace being unique. However, through honest self-reflection, without the judgment of what you "should" do, you can uncover what will really work best for you.*

I have many clients who are night owls. Every single one of them has told me they feel they should wake up earlier. There is a belief that successful or productive people start their mornings early, so they try it, and it rarely works. Why? Their natural tendency is to stay up late. They have extra energy and are at their best later in the day. When

I convince them to try using that natural boost to their advantage, they always end up feeling happier. Let go of what you think you *should* do and explore what really works best.

To guide you a bit further, I've included some questions below. If you are interested in going even deeper, do a search for "know yourself better questions," and many links will be listed with various questions for you to consider. Spending a little bit of time on this now will save you lots of time later. Knowledge of yourself allows you to eliminate some of the hacks in this book in favor of others that are more likely to work. Having to do less trial and error will lead to more time saved!

Here are some of my favorite questions:

- *Are you an introvert or extrovert?*

    Knowing this helps you manage your energy levels. If you are an introvert, you will need quiet time by yourself—or with very few people—to recharge before expecting to start on a project.

- *Are you an early bird or night owl?*

    When do you have the most physical and mental energy during the day? When are you most productive? Plan to work on your passion project accordingly.

- *What do you enjoy doing that makes you lose track of time?*

    Do more of this! This kind of task or project will boost your energy.

- *What skills come naturally to you?*

    Using your strengths and talents can boost motivation and confidence.

- *What is working well in your life right now? What is not?*

    Being curious about this will allow you to begin to let go of the tasks that may be holding you back from starting on your passion project.

Is ADHD Part of Your Story?

Knowing your strengths and tendencies can provide guidance on the best strategies for getting started. In addition, another aspect of knowing yourself is to learn more about your neurodivergence. Understanding this unique aspect of your brain is very helpful with figuring out the strategies that will best support you.

If ADHD or other learning and attention issues are a part of your life, understanding how that impacts you can offer forgiveness for the past and hope for the future, as well as specific ways to get stuff done. Clients often tell me that an ADHD diagnosis helped them understand lifelong behaviors. As they learned more about what ADHD is and isn't, they were able to identify specific examples of how it had impacted their lives. More importantly, they were able avoid some of those pitfalls moving forward.

One client shared that her ADHD diagnosis helped her understand why she did so well in school but fell apart later in life when she had a job and family.

She learned she needed a more structured day with outer accountability in order to stay organized, show up to appointments on time, and complete tasks. In addition, she saw the strengths of having ADHD and how they had positively impacted her life. Her passion, creativity, and curiosity, all part of having ADHD, had inspired a fulfilling career. She was able to forgive herself for some mistakes she had made in her twenties and move forward in life with greater success.

Increasing your understanding of how ADHD, autism, executive functions, etc. impact your life is one of the most important things you can do for yourself if you want more success and happiness. You need to educate yourself. However, I want to be clear that pursuing an official diagnosis is a very personal decision. Pursuing a diagnosis might be part of your exploration process or, for various reasons, it might not. Many people share with me that they don't see the point in pursuing a diagnosis because they do not want to take medication. If this is true for you, please know that a diagnosis can provide so much more. There are many ways to treat neurodivergent conditions, and medication is only one of them. The assessment process itself may be worth it. The process can open your eyes to all the ways ADHD has been a positive aspect in your life and begin to change your mindset around what you believe you can accomplish.

Whether you decide to pursue an official diagnosis or not, I encourage you to, at the very least, explore how learning and attention issues impact your life. Do some reading, talk to others, and find support resources specific to neurodivergent people. When you know yourself—what works and what doesn't and *why*—you can start to choose strategies that work. When you uncover the strengths of having ADHD, you can tap into them for greater success. As you start to accomplish the smaller tasks with consistency (laundry, for example), you realize the bigger stuff is also possible.

ADHD and other learning and attention issues often get a bad rap. They can be very complex, and there are many emotions around them, along with the facts. What if we were to shift our mindset, ditch our feelings about it, and look at it as simply a label? Knowing you have ADHD can help you understand yourself. It is an explanation, and as such, it can support you in creating your best life.

If you have ADHD or think you might, I encourage you to read more about the ADHD journey in the following section. Through my work with students, parents, and clients, I've identified three phases people go through as they live a life with learning and attention issues. See if you can identify where you are at, if this applies to you. Knowing where you are on this journey may help you identify the next steps on your path to success and happiness.

The ADHD Journey

Living

In the first phase of the ADHD journey, you don't even realize you have it. You are merely living your life to the best of your ability. Perhaps you are wondering why you feel different from others, and you feel frustrated when you notice that those around you seem to have an easier time in school, at work, or with maintaining relationships.

Beginning in early childhood, kids who have ADHD receive many more negative messages than those who do not. They are often told they are hyper, lazy, chatty, forgetful, or spacey. A common message is they don't meet their potential. They hear the words "no" or "stop that" frequently throughout the day.

Even at a young age, kids come up with coping mechanisms to help them make it through the day. Folders and reminder lists can support organization so assignments are completed and turned in on time. Sports or hobbies lead to friendships and may help to calm an active mind and body.

Despite the ways kids learn to cope, school and friendships often remain difficult. As they grow older, they may feel broken, left out, and unloved. Living with ADHD as an adult can be better because you get to choose your career and no longer have to work on something that is boring and uninteresting.

However, it may also be worse as you balance living on your own with a job and a household to manage.

Learning

Somewhere along life's journey, most people start to learn more about themselves. It may be a deliberate effort to read, watch, and learn new strategies to support success or you may haphazardly discover systems that make your life easier. Sometimes a loved one, friend, or teacher may make suggestions that impact your life for the better.

In the early stages of the learning phase, you may go through a bit of trial and error. You may unknowingly discover that a certain type of planner works best for you as you try out the different options.

People stumble across meditation or yoga and realize it benefits them. Others find apps that can keep them focused, on time, and organized. You instinctively keep what works and ditch the rest!

For many people, they find what works and may never even know (or need to know) they actually have ADHD.

Others may purposely begin down a path of self-discovery. Some people may seek out medical advice and a diagnosis. Others may conduct research, read articles, or watch videos to learn more about ADHD. ADHD is complex, and as you learn more, you will likely identify which aspects you can and cannot relate to.

The learning phase may continue for the rest of your life—discovering new information, trying out new ideas, identifying new strategies. However, I believe that in order to live your best life, you need to move to phase three, which is loving yourself.

Loving

ADHD is a label. It is not who you are, and it is not a bad thing. Knowing you have ADHD can help you make sense of yourself in much the same way as taking a personality assessment. Ditch the negative feelings and connotations of having ADHD and use it as a tool for understanding yourself. Phase three is all about embracing your ADHD!

In all the learning that you did in the previous phase, you likely came across the many strengths of ADHD—being creative, resilient, inventive, entertaining, adaptable, authentic, passionate, smart, and resourceful. There are many positives to having ADHD! Many people think that having ADHD is a gift.

So, what do you do when the "icky" side of ADHD shows up in your life? People who love themselves still become frustrated, they still forget things, and they have bad days. However, they don't let these things define them.

Embracing your ADHD requires a bit of a mindset shift. After a bad day, acknowledge it, recognize it as a part of being human, and be kind to yourself. Remember that for as many ways that ADHD may bring you down, there are as many (maybe more) ways it lifts you up.

Identify the ADHD traits that make you unique. Implement the strategies that lead to your success. Own your power! Embrace ADHD and love yourself.

Journal Prompts

Remember, slowing down and taking a moment to write down your thoughts will make it more likely for you to get started. For this chapter, I encourage you to choose at least one of the following prompts and write out your answers to learn more about yourself. Pull out your paper or notebook if you need more space.

Choose a personality framework and take an assessment. What did you learn about yourself that might help you start your project?

Choose two self-discovery questions to answer here. How might this knowledge help you stop procrastinating?

Where are you at on your ADHD Journey (if this applies to you)? If you are looking to move to the next step, what action do you need to take?

CHAPTER 4
Navigating the Hacks

This chapter will be short. I know you are ready to jump in with the hacks and try them out. Before you do, I want to provide an overview of what you'll find, as well as some suggestions to think about as you move forward.

This chapter will continue to help you narrow down which hacks to try first and give you some tips on what to watch for as you explore the hacks.

Types of Hacks

You could choose any hack, and it might help you get started. However, if you are interested in saving some time, I'd like you to consider *why* you can't get started (see Chapter 2) and what you know will work for *you* (see Chapter 3). These insights will help guide you to the most effective type of hack.

There are four types of hacks. I've provided a very brief overview here and more context for each in the subsequent chapters. Though the four categories don't directly correspond to the reasons for not getting started (because our procrastination is often a tangled web of reasons), there is some overlap. Busy-ness, distractibility, feelings of overwhelm, and lack of motivation can each be addressed in different ways. Often, one hack is good for multiple reasons. Consider the four types of hacks listed below and decide where you want to start.

Accountability Hacks

Remember, we tend to react and complete tasks that feel urgent, sometimes at the expense of the important things in our lives. Our dreams and passion projects are usually quite important, but they're not urgent. Accountability hacks purposely engineer urgency into the situation, so your brain will feel ready to get started. These hacks will work well when you are busy, distracted, or need a quick boost of motivation. *See Chapter 5 for Accountability Hacks.*

Energy Hacks

It is so much harder to get started and remain focused when you are dragging. We sometimes need a quick boost to our energy levels, but at other times, we need to focus on our overall health. Healthy habits such as eating, exercise, and sleep also play a role in your ability to begin a task. Some energy hacks will work well if you are distracted or looking for a quick boost of motivation, and others will support you for sustained motivation. *See Chapter 6 for Energy Hacks.*

Clarity Hacks

Feeling overwhelmed with a task? When you have a larger project with multiple steps, or when you need to learn something new, it can feel hard to start. If this is the case for you, you might need to put a little more thought into *how* to complete a project. What are the steps? What needs to happen first? These hacks will help you organize your thoughts and have clarity on how to begin. They will lessen your feelings of overwhelm to help you get started. *See Chapter 7 for Clarity Hacks.*

Mindset Hacks

Don't underestimate the power of your mind! Remember the old adage? If you think you can, you can. If you think you can't, you can't. Our thoughts have a huge impact on our ability to get started. While energy hacks give a boost to your body, mindset hacks give a boost to your brain. Choose a mindset hack if you are overwhelmed or looking for overall, sustained motivation. *See Chapter 8 for Mindset Hacks.*

How to Approach the Hacks

You should always do what works for you. In that spirit, the way to progress through the second half of this book will be different for everyone. I give you permission to read this book out of order! Bounce around or skim through the hacks until you find one that jumps out at you. You might have a particular task in mind and be looking for the perfect hack for that task. You might prefer to have an overview of all the hacks, a general knowledge of them to pull from when needed. Whatever your preference, read the hacks in a way that works for you. Here are some suggestions.

Read Them All

You might want to read every hack all the way through before trying any of them. Doing this will give you a good sense of the variety of choices, and you can circle back to the ones you like best. An overview can provide you with the clarity you need to make the best choice the next time you need to get started.

Try Them One at a Time

Another option is to read and try each hack one by one. Read the first hack and try the first hack—rinse and repeat. Every day we must get started on something. Dishes, getting the car's oil changed, cleaning a closet, writing a paper, making a phone call—the tasks never really end. Choose one hack to try each day until you've cycled through all 50. Make note of what works and what doesn't for everyday tasks so you can identify your favorites and use them to begin your passion project. You might be surprised by one that works well for you.

Skim for Your Favorites

After reading Chapters 1–3, you will have a good sense of where to start. Perhaps you resonate with one of the examples I shared and want to jump right to that hack for your own task. Trust your gut and skim for the hacks you already know are likely to work best for you.

Explore a Specific Type

Remember, there are four types of hacks: Accountability (Chapter 5), Energy (Chapter 6), Clarity (Chapter 7), and Mindset (Chapter 8). Do you already know which one you need? Jump ahead to that chapter and get started. You can always explore the others later.

Common Pitfalls

This is the section of the book where I remind you it's not always going to be easy. Just as it hasn't been a piece of cake up to this point, I doubt that the first hack you choose will be the magic answer. When you have ADHD or other learning and attention issues, you might be a bit impulsive. Although it's completely okay to jump ahead and try out a hack that has resonated with you, I also want to set you up for success.

Check out my story which illustrates many of the pitfalls you should be aware of.

When I first had the idea for this book, I tried Hack #8 and shared my plan to write a book with others. I was sure that this one simple hack was what would get me started. It didn't work, so I organized my thoughts using Hack #28. This prompted me to do some writing for a month or so until I lost momentum. The project went on the back burner. Despite my love of writing, I started to question my ability and my desire. Who was I to write a book anyway? So, I focused on Hack #36 to shift my mindset around my belief that I could actually do this project. Meanwhile, I remembered the hack type that almost always works best for me—accountability—so I set some up by hiring a book coach (Hack #3). That's when I truly started making progress.

What are you going to do (and think) if the first or second hack doesn't work for you as it didn't for me? Choosing the best hack and getting started right away, every time, is rare, as you learned from my story. My own experience and my work with students and clients have made me aware of the stumbling blocks that trip us up and potentially kill off passion projects. When you are aware of them ahead of time, you can avoid leaving your project on the back burner for too long. You've gotten this far, so keep reading to be sure you don't fall into one of these four common traps.

The Magic Answer

A common pitfall is the belief that one hack will be the magic answer, like when I tried Hack #8 (Share First) at the start of writing this book. Most often it's a combination of hacks that gets you started. You can try one at a time but pay attention to the combination of hacks that works best. It will likely be one or two from each category. You may start off needing one, a clarity hack for example, and then need to add another, such as a mindset hack, later.

One and Done

Another pitfall is to give up when the first or second attempt doesn't work. I want you to go into this knowing it will probably take a few tries before you identify the hack(s) that work best for you. For my clients and me, there's always a bit (or even a lot) of trial and error. In my story, you learned that I had to try a few hacks before I found the ones that worked. Try what you think will work, but don't let it derail you if it doesn't. Don't give up if the first hack doesn't work. Restart as many times as you need to!

I Can't, I Shouldn't

Never forget how powerful your mind is. I've said this before, and I'll say it again. If you believe you can, you can, but if you believe you can't, you can't. Our brains tend to be very judgmental. If your thoughts are filled with, "I shouldn't do that," or, "I can't possibly figure this out," or, "That will never work for me," you won't get very far.

Almost everyone, including me (see my story above), is doubtful at some point. Be sure to try out the hacks with curiosity. When something doesn't work, instead of letting it beat you down, be curious and consider why it didn't work. This will often lead you to the next step. Choose curiosity over judgment!

I Forget

One of the most common phrases I hear is, "I totally forgot to try that!" Just as I forgot how well accountability works for me, my clients often identify a hack that works well for them and a few weeks or months later, perhaps with a new project, they forget to use it again. I've included space next to each hack in this book for you to take notes and mark the ones that work best for you. This way, you'll only have to remember to look back at the book.

You are ready! You've tapped into your passion around your projects and dreams. You've considered why you haven't been able to get started. You've learned a bit (or possibly a lot) about yourself. You are aware of the pitfalls.

The next four chapters include 50 hacks to help you get started. Each chapter corresponds to a different type of hack: Accountability, Energy, Clarity, and Mindset. I've included some extra details about when each type of hack could be useful.

It's time to jump into the hacks and *get started*! I believe in you!

CHAPTER 5
Accountability Hacks

When I launched my coaching business, I found it nearly impossible to sit down and write.

It was so perplexing. I love writing! I've always loved writing. In school, the research papers were finished without an issue. While I was teaching, I enjoyed writing progress reports for my students. Why was writing for my business so hard?

For a while, I thought I simply didn't have the time. So many other tasks needed to get done, and my clients came first. I also blamed a lack of inspiration and ideas, but that wasn't entirely true. I'm always thinking of new content.

And then it hit me.

Those research papers and progress reports had a deadline, which offered a sense of urgency. Someone was always expecting to see them when they were complete. Accountability was built in. That was the missing piece in my coaching business! When we are the boss, we often lose the outer expectations that worked so well for us in the past. Aren't we all the bosses of our own lives? As adults, we make all the decisions about our schedules and what has to get done. There are so many tasks we need to complete that are important but not urgent, and there's rarely anyone overseeing us as there was when we were younger. Our passion projects, though important, are entirely up to us to complete.

Gretchen Rubin, author, podcaster, and speaker, writes about accountability in her book, *The Four Tendencies*. The "obliger," one of the tendencies she describes, is someone who resists inner expectations, such as a goal they have set for themselves like working out three times per week. However, they meet outer expectations (goals that involve others) such as going to a group class at the gym three times per week. Both involve the goal of increased exercise, but the first is something you expect of yourself, and the second involves other people. For the obliger, accountability is the key. They struggle to work on goals that are more personal, such as sticking with a daily exercise routine or making progress on a passion project, unless someone is counting on them or checking in with them.

This describes me perfectly. I have many ideas about projects and habits, both personally and professionally, that I'd like to work on. However, if no one is watching, they simply don't happen. If I decide I'm going to begin exercising each day, it won't happen unless I have a partner. An inner expectation to publish blog posts every month also isn't going to happen, unless someone is waiting to see them. Anything I declare as a self-imposed expectation won't happen, unless I set up accountability and create a sense of urgency with additional outer expectations.

I was lucky to stumble across someone else who was in the same boat. She asked if we could be accountability partners. For a while, we sent each other a list of our weekly tasks and reported back on our progress at the end of each week. It was amazing! I accomplished so much. I discovered the power of accountability.

When this partnership ended, I found it challenging to start it up with someone else. I had two limiting beliefs that I have also heard from many clients. First, I thought to myself that I should be able to do this without someone else checking in with me. Then I thought that asking someone else to check in with me is such a bother.

One key to getting past these beliefs is to drop self-judgment. Needing outer accountability is no different than being an introvert or preferring chocolate ice cream. It is simply who you are. When you accept it as a natural part of your personality and stop resisting it, you'll have an easier time figuring out what type of accountability you need to get started and get things done.

Please don't think you have to go out and find an accountability partner to check in with you every day. There are countless ways to create urgency and accountability in your life without "bothering" someone else. Whether or not you're an obliger, all you need is a willingness to try a few of the following hacks and look at the results with curiosity. You'll find the ones that work for you and will be magically transformed. Not only will you get started on tricky tasks and passion projects, but you'll also get them done.

Hacks #1-8

For each of the following hacks, I've provided space for you to take notes. If you try out the hack, be sure to take a moment and write down the result. Rank the hack on a scale of 1–5, with 1 meaning "it did not work at all" and 5 meaning "I started right away."

Write down the task or project you started, and, if needed, note anything that may help you to know yourself better or use this hack in the future. Later, when you've forgotten what works and what doesn't, you'll thank yourself for those notes!

Get Started Hack #1
Go to a Virtual Work Session

Believe it or not, even before we were all aware of Zoom, virtual work sessions existed, and they are quite a powerful motivator. They vary in length and complexity, but they all include you sharing what you'll be working on, working on it "side-by-side" with others virtually, and reporting on your progress at the end. Do a web search, ask around, or come join me for a Power Hour (check my website for dates and times: www.barbhubbardcoaching.com) and get started.

Task or project started:

On a scale of 1–5, how did it work for you?
1   2   3   4   5

Notes

Get Started Hack #2
Collaborate with a Partner

Find someone who has a similar goal or project and work together. Create a product, plan a presentation, or work out together. Often, you can each use your strengths to come together in a new and exciting way, and the end result will benefit you both! When you work with a partner, you'll get started.

Task or project started:

On a scale of 1–5, how did it work for you?
1   2   3   4   5

Notes

Get Started Hack #3
Hire Support People

Sometimes we need help to do something not in our area of expertise. Consider hiring support to keep you accountable. Want to get started on your taxes? Hire a CPA. Want to take the next step in your business? Hire a business coach. Want to publish a blog post? Hire an assistant who will be waiting for your content. Even if you can do it, hire support to be sure you will do it. It's a win-win-win. You get started on a task, they get paid, and you make progress toward your dreams.

Task or project started:

On a scale of 1–5, how did it work for you?
1   2   3   4   5

Notes

Get Started Hack #4
Schedule First

Have you ever noticed that the best motivation to clean your house is to invite friends over for dinner? If you have an amazing idea for an event, choose a date and mark it on your calendar. Share it on social media and tell everyone you know. Now get to work! Scheduling first will give you the urgency and accountability to get started.

Task or project started:

On a scale of 1–5, how did it work for you?
1 2 3 4 5

Notes

Get Started Hack #5
Ask for a Deadline

If you've ever been on a committee or worked on a group project, you've sat in a meeting where everyone is given the next task. Usually, a manager will provide a due date, and you know they'll be checking in. It's easier to get started on this task. Sometimes, however, someone will ask for a favor and say, "Whenever you have time." It doesn't feel urgent, so it's harder to get started. So, ask for a deadline! Having a deadline will give you the motivation to get started.

Task or project started:	Notes
On a scale of 1–5, how did it work for you? 1 2 3 4 5	

Get Started Hack #6
Reward Yourself

It is natural to want to complete tasks for rewards. Most people work for the incentive of a paycheck. We are rewarded with a "thank you" or kind words when we help others. We prepare a meal for the enjoyment of eating it. With a task that is tricky to start, try attaching a reward to it. Decide ahead of time that you will buy a new outfit, have a peaceful cup of tea, or call a friend when you are finished. Rewards don't have to be expensive or take a lot of time. Simple pleasures can help you get started.

Task or project started:

On a scale of 1–5, how did it work for you?
1 2 3 4 5

Notes

Get Started Hack #7
Sprint

Many people love competition. They push themselves further when they are trying to beat someone else or set a new record. If no one else is around, compete with yourself! Take a look at your task, consider how fast you've accomplished it in the past, and set a time limit for its completion. How much can you get done in a certain number of minutes? Can you beat your record? This urgency may be the push you need to get started.

Task or project started:

On a scale of 1–5, how did it work for you?
1 2 3 4 5

Notes

Get Started Hack #8
Share First

Social media can be a trap. We can get sucked in and waste time scrolling. However, the connection to others can also be helpful, so make it work for you! Choose a task you have been putting off and tell others you'll post pictures when you've started (or completed) a task. You'll feel like someone is checking in on you, creating the urgency to get started. However, the onus is on you to follow up, so you don't have to worry about "bothering" anyone else. Share on social media and get started.

Task or project started:

On a scale of 1–5, how did it work for you?
1   2   3   4   5

Notes

CHAPTER 6

Energy Hacks

Our lives are busy. For most people reading this book, I'd be willing to bet that every minute of your day is full, and by the end of the day, you have little energy left. It's a wonder that you are reading this book. And when you feel tired or drained, you're less likely to get started on most things, let alone your passion project. So, even if you have an extra hour, how do you find the energy to get started?

Create it. Yes, you can create the energy you need to get started. The hacks below are designed for this purpose.

When my kids were younger, my days were filled with teaching full time, driving to sports practices, making dinner, and overseeing homework. Most nights, I was asleep before my head even hit the pillow. In general, if you had asked me to squeeze in one more task, even something I loved doing, I would have said you were crazy. I had no energy left for anything extra. However, if a friend happened to call or if my family decided to play with the dogs in the backyard, I suddenly had a second wind. My spirits were lifted, my energy stores were replenished, and I had the energy to do much more than usual.

Moving your body and doing fun and healthy activities allows you to generate additional energy, and you can do it at any time of day.

If you're having a sluggish day, managing your energy is often the key to getting started. There are many different ways to do this. That's why this is the longest chapter of hacks. I've subdivided the energy hacks into three categories: Move Your Body, Do What You Love, and Power Up Your Healthy Habits.

I provide a brief description of each before diving into the hacks themselves.

Hacks #9–26

For each of the hacks in the following sections, I've included some space for you to take notes. If you try out the hack, be sure to take a moment and write down the result. Rank the hack on a scale of 1–5, with 1 meaning "it did not work at all" and 5 meaning "I started right away."

Write down the task or project you started, and, if needed, note anything that may help you to know yourself better or use this hack in the future.

Later, when you've forgotten what works and what doesn't, you'll thank yourself for those notes!

Move Your Body – Hacks #9–15

Sitting behind a desk all day is draining. Running from place to place and task to task can be exhausting, but if a project is important to us, it is possible to find the energy to get started.

Sometimes, we first need to dig deep to find or create a little bit of energy. Movement is a quick and easy way to make this happen.

Get Started Hack #9
Switch Seats

Get a new perspective by sitting in a different chair. Move to the other side of the table, move into the sun, be near your pets, or sit away from the window. After you've shifted to a new location, take a fresh look at the task in front of you. It will seem new and easy! When my kids were in elementary school, they did their homework at the kitchen table. When they became too distracted, I had them move to the other side of the table, and just like that, they were back on task.

Task or project started:

On a scale of 1–5, how did it work for you?
1 2 3 4 5

Notes

Get Started Hack #10
Change Your Scenery

Move to a new location. Sometimes we need a completely new environment around us. Sit in your backyard or on the front porch. Lay on the floor, or prop yourself up in your bed or on the couch. Other options are coffee shops, parks, a friend's house, and, my personal favorite, sitting in your car! Change your scenery and get started!

Task or project started:

On a scale of 1–5, how did it work for you?
1 2 3 4 5

Notes

Get Started Hack #11
Go for a Walk

Walk around the block, walk around your yard, walk around your home, or simply walk in place. Walking clears your head and gets the blood flowing to your brain to energize you. As few as 50 steps ought to do it, which takes no time at all. Go for a walk and then get started!

Task or project started:

Notes

On a scale of 1–5, how did it work for you?
1 2 3 4 5

Get Started Hack #12
Do Jumping Jacks

Remember doing jumping jacks as a warm-up in physical education class? Try it as a warm-up for your next task. Of course, you can substitute push-ups, marching in place, sit-ups, or even planking. The idea is to take your mind off of things for a couple of minutes and get your blood flowing. It's a great hack when you have very little space or very little time. Choose a warm-up exercise and get started!

Task or project started:

Notes

On a scale of 1–5, how did it work for you?
1 2 3 4 5

Get Started Hack #13
Move While Working

One of my favorite ways to increase my productivity is to walk while I work. I walk while talking on the phone, dictating a message, and brainstorming ideas. The movement inspires great thoughts, and it is easier to get started. A twist on this is to sit in a swivel chair, a chair with wheels, or a rocking chair. You can also purchase or create a standing desk. Move while working to get started!

Task or project started:

On a scale of 1–5, how did it work for you?
1 2 3 4 5

Notes

Get Started Hack #14
Gather Your Supplies

It can be distracting to keep getting up to find the materials needed for a task. Gathering everything beforehand keeps us focused and may provide a spark to get started. Pens, paper, highlighters, books, laptop, snacks, water, etc. may all be in different locations. Collecting your supplies will boost your energy. And this hack serves a double purpose. As you think about the task and needed supplies, you also think through the task and organize your thoughts, which is also helpful to get started!

Task or project started:

On a scale of 1–5, how did it work for you?
1 2 3 4 5

Notes

Get Started Hack #15
Dance

Have a few extra minutes? Turn on your favorite, upbeat song and start dancing. Sing along! Music can boost your energy and shift your mood in an instant. Add in the movement of dancing, and it will provide the quick boost of energy you need to get started!

Task or project started:

On a scale of 1–5, how did it work for you?
1   2   3   4   5

Notes

Do What You Love – Hacks #16–21

Our body gets energy from food, rest, and movement, and this physical energy is necessary if you want to get started on your passion project. However, our *minds* can also be energized, which can provide the motivation to get started.

Have you ever had a meeting that dragged on and on? You watched the clock and couldn't believe how slowly the hour progressed. You felt bored and drained and frustrated. Perhaps you continued to feel sluggish for much of the day. You're not likely to get started on your projects when you're feeling like this.

Conversely, have you ever had a conversation with someone, and suddenly the hour was over? You were so engrossed in the interaction that the time flew by. You felt excited and energized. You felt as though you could conquer the world, and you carried this energy through the rest of your day, resulting in massive productivity.

In both examples, you had the same hour of time—sixty minutes—right? Yet, the energy you felt was a huge factor in how the next block of time could be used.

Think again about a situation when the time flew by. How did you feel? Were you with someone you loved to be around? Were you doing an activity you love? Were you helping a loved one? Were you checking off to-do list items?

Just as we can boost our physical energy with rest, nutritious foods, or movement, we also can boost our mental energy with happiness, love, and success. These emotions play a pivotal role in getting started. The hacks in this section are designed to energize your mind.

Get Started Hack #16
Have Fun First

Too often we wait to do the fun stuff until after we complete a task. We feel as though our hobbies are indulgent, and it's selfish to spend time on them. Sometimes it can be motivating to look forward to spending time playing a game or working on a puzzle. However, fun activities boost our energy, so why not try having fun first? Do something you love for five to ten minutes, and let the positive energy fill you up. It will stick with you for a while and motivate you to get started!

Task or project started:

On a scale of 1–5, how did it work for you?
1 2 3 4 5

Notes

Get Started Hack #17
Be Generous

Generosity can leave us feeling good for hours, and when we feel good, we have the energy to do the hard stuff. I have a friend who likes to send greeting cards to random people, simply to brighten their day. She keeps a stash of cards in her office. Prior to a harder task, she sits down and writes out a message to someone, and she addresses and stamps the card to go out later in the day. What generous act can you do to boost your energy and get started?

Task or project started:

On a scale of 1–5, how did it work for you?
1   2   3   4   5

Notes

Get Started Hack #18
Build Momentum

Popular advice tells you that when you are ready to work, you should jump right into the hardest, most difficult thing. For some people, this works. For me and many others, this approach backfires. When I can't start the bigger stuff, I sit and stew about it, which lowers my energy, making it difficult to do anything. Instead, try working on a few tiny tasks first, the type of tasks that take a few minutes each. As you cross them off your list, you will bring that momentum into bigger, more complex projects.

Task or project started:	Notes
On a scale of 1–5, how did it work for you? 1 2 3 4 5	

Get Started Hack #19
Work at a Different Time of Day

We all have a preferred time of day when we are most productive. Some of us are morning people, and others are night owls. At what time of day do you have the most energy? Plan to work on your hard tasks then. You'll be able to get things done faster. Don't try to write a paper first thing in the morning if you are a night owl. Choose the best time of day for you and get started!

Task or project started:

On a scale of 1–5, how did it work for you?
1 2 3 4 5

Notes

Get Started Hack #20
Tap Into Your Creative Side

Are you a creative person? Do you love to play with words? Do you love and appreciate color, organization, or shapes? For many people, doing something creative is an energy booster. Consider how to make your task more creative. Are you able to add an element of creativity to make it more enjoyable? Tap into your creative side and get started!

Task or project started:

Notes

On a scale of 1–5, how did it work for you?
1   2   3   4   5

Get Started Hack #21
Plan a Strategic Work Hour

Think about what brings you joy—a warm bath, a cup of coffee, mentoring, writing, public speaking, time with a loved one, calling a friend—the list is endless. These joyful activities energize you. Choose a few that you do (or could do) each week. Plan to do a more difficult brain-consuming task immediately after doing one (or more) of the things that bring you joy. Take advantage of the energy boost. Strategically plan a work hour and get started!

Task or project started:

On a scale of 1–5, how did it work for you?
1 2 3 4 5

Notes

Power Up Your Healthy Habits – Hacks #22–26

When it comes to getting started, we often simply need a quick boost of motivation. A burst of energy can push us past the starting line, and from there we are good to go.

However, you may not be able to rely on these short bursts all the time. For the getting started hacks to work consistently, you will also need a solid foundation.

As with the foundation of a house, a baseline of energy is necessary for everything else to work. The pipes and electrical lines support the fun light fixtures and custom-made bathtubs. The walls provide a structure to hang your favorite pictures. Without the foundation, you couldn't easily flip on a light or grab a glass of water, and your home would be no less than a heap of disorganized ideas.

When your to-do list and calendar look like a cluttered mess, and the quick hacks aren't working, consider your foundation—your healthy habits.

We all know that we need to eat healthy, move our bodies, and get enough sleep. Too often, we push these needs aside because we simply need to get a task done. And then the next and the next and the next. Before you know it, you are holed up in your office for 12 hours and eating junk food. Sound familiar? No wonder the hacks aren't working!

Before you reach for the next quick fix, consider your healthy habits. Strengthen them. Focus on choosing healthy foods, getting adequate rest, and moving your body each day. I promise that the time it takes to do this will save you time in the long run. You'll get started more easily on that next task.

Taking the time to create healthy habits may seem like a lot of work, and I'm not going to tell you that it isn't. It is! But it's one hundred percent worth it. With a solid foundation, the quick motivation hacks are more likely to work, and everything will seem easier. Each of the following hacks may offer a boost in the moment, but if developed as a foundational habit or routine, they'll provide an even greater benefit of sustained motivation.

Get Started Hack #22
Eat a Healthy Snack

Feeling frustrated with your productivity? Check in with yourself. Did you forget to eat? This hack is beneficial for two reasons. First, you will end up moving your body, which is a natural energizer. Second, that healthy snack will give your body the energy it needs to refocus and get started on your next task. To make this a habit, set a timer to remind you in the middle of each day to eat a healthy snack, and get started!

Task or project started:

On a scale of 1–5, how did it work for you?
1 2 3 4 5

Notes

Get Started Hack #23
Go to Sleep

Trying to create more time by staying up later or getting up earlier can leave us tired. Instead, choose a reasonable bedtime. You'll likely feel ready to get started after only one day. Try this for two to three weeks, and you'll notice an even bigger difference. Adequate rest provides energy you need to be productive. Instead of cramming in one more task late in the day, you'll accomplish things faster and more accurately throughout the day. It will also create a foundation for other hacks to work.

Task or project started:	Notes
On a scale of 1–5, how did it work for you? 1 2 3 4 5	

Get Started Hack #24
Take a Nap

Your body gives you a signal when it needs a break. Too often, we ignore this. Feeling unfocused? Eyes drooping and irritated? You need rest! Walk away from your task and lie down for 15 minutes. After a quick nap, you'll be back to work in no time. You'll end up saving time in the long run. When you notice yourself feeling drained or sleepy, take a nap. With practice, you'll start to notice this before you've wasted too much time, and it will become a regular habit for you.

Task or project started:

On a scale of 1–5, how did it work for you?
1   2   3   4   5

Notes

Get Started Hack #25
Meditate

Often, when feeling sluggish, taking a short (3–5 minute) pause to regroup is all you need. It's a chance to reflect and can help you refocus on the most important tasks. Having a regular, daily meditation practice creates a habit of pausing. Choose a time that works in your schedule, turn on one of the many free meditation apps, and spend a few minutes clearing your mind. Taking time to do this each day will allow you to be more focused throughout your day and week.

Task or project started:

On a scale of 1–5, how did it work for you?
1   2   3   4   5

Notes

Get Started Hack #26
Take a Breath

No time to meditate? Take a breath. This simple, quick hack offers a lot of bang for your buck. It forces you to pause, if only for a moment. It clears your mind and allows you to refocus, and you always have time to breathe. If this works for you, you can start to build in a practice of deep breathing. There are countless breathing techniques available, and any of them would be a valuable piece to your foundation of healthy habits. Take a breath and get started!

Task or project started:

Notes

On a scale of 1–5, how did it work for you?
1 2 3 4 5

CHAPTER 7

Clarity Hacks

I believe that one of the most common reasons people procrastinate is because they are overwhelmed by a project. The project seems too big, and they don't know where to start. There may be many steps, a lot of information to organize, or other people involved in the project. They may have something new to learn, which often feels scary.

Our brains like to keep us safe, so if there is any fear of something being too hard, too complicated, or any chance of embarrassment or failure, our brain will pump the brakes and come up with all kinds of reasons not to get started. For many of us, our brains *overcomplicate and overthink everything*! When it comes to starting the next task, we get stuck.

It's okay to feel this way, *and* it's okay to move past it. We don't need to give up and remain stuck. Often, a few minutes organizing our thoughts is all it takes. When we've figured out the first step and have clarity regarding the end result, the middle will usually work itself out.

The truth of the matter is that our dreams and passion projects *are* probably a bit complicated. Also, there's likely some risk in putting ourselves out there and certainly a fear of failure.

But it's worth it.

Your passion project is going to help at least one other person, if not many. It's going to improve lives. It is something you need to start!

When you catch your brain going in a thousand different directions, telling you all the reasons not to start, remind yourself how important this is to you and others, and tell your brain that you are only going to focus on one step at a time. Tell it to stop overcomplicating everything in its effort to slow you down. Find clarity on where to start by trying one of these hacks.

Hacks #27–35

For each of the hacks below, I've included some space for you to take notes. If you try out the hack, be sure to take a moment and write down the result.

Rank the hack on a scale of 1–5, with 1 meaning "it did not work at all" and 5 meaning "I started right away."

Write down the task or project you started, and, if needed, note anything that may help you to know yourself better or use this hack in the future. Later, when you've forgotten what works and what doesn't, you'll thank yourself for those notes!

Get Started Hack #27
Draw It

Many people think in pictures, so when they are surrounded by words, lengthy books, and audio podcasts, things may feel overwhelming. If you are a visual learner, it may be helpful to draw out the plans for your project. Somewhat like a comic strip or graphic novel, draw a picture of each step. This can help you find clarity around the project, and it will also be useful to refer back to throughout the work. Draw it and get started!

Task or project started:

On a scale of 1–5, how did it work for you?
1 2 3 4 5

Notes

Get Started Hack #28
Make a List

When we have a lot going on in our lives and multiple steps to complete for a project, we also have a lot of ideas floating around in our heads. It can be helpful to simplify those thoughts by creating a list. You can use bullet points or create an outline, but the idea is to write down only single words or short phrases. Get the ideas out of your head and organize them to clarify what you need to do first, second, third, etc. Make a list and get started!

Task or project started:

On a scale of 1–5, how did it work for you?
1 2 3 4 5

Notes

Get Started Hack #29
Write It Out

Separate from writing a list or outlining your plans, it's can be helpful to write out your thoughts and feelings. Journaling can be done on your computer or phone; it doesn't have to be in an actual journal. Find a quiet place and consider a few questions. What am I feeling about this project? Why do I feel overwhelmed? What's really holding me back? These prompts may help you clarify your feelings and let go of what could be holding you back. Write it out and get started!

Task or project started:

On a scale of 1–5, how did it work for you?
1   2   3   4   5

Notes

Get Started Hack #30
Visualize

If you have a complex project, it can help to visualize the individual steps involved. Close your eyes, take some deep breaths to clear your mind, and picture each step until you have a final project in your mind's eye. If it's a physical project, think about the colors, visual elements, and each piece in its place. If it's a writing project, conjure up the image of having all the words written as you hand the final piece to your boss or client. Picture the smiles, feel the joy of completion, open your eyes, and get started!

Task or project started:

On a scale of 1–5, how did it work for you?
1 2 3 4 5

Notes

Get Started Hack #31
Talk About It

Many women I work with process their thoughts out loud. Unfortunately, most people also spend a lot of time caught up in their own heads. There's power in "talking it out." Find a friend, colleague, or coach and share that you are having trouble getting started. Talk through the details of the project and the steps needed for completion. Are you unable to find someone when you need them? Record your thoughts. Through conversation, you'll gain clarity, and you'll be ready and motivated to get started!

Task or project started:	Notes
On a scale of 1–5, how did it work for you? 1 2 3 4 5	

Get Started Hack #32
Know Your "Why"

Sometimes, when a project feels complicated, we get caught up in the details and forget our original purpose. We may not want to fill out meaningless paperwork or learn a new skill, but it is essential to the completion of the project. Pause and get clear about your "why." Why is it important to you to complete this task? If you complete it, what is the greater good? Know your why and get started!

Task or project started:

On a scale of 1–5, how did it work for you?
1 2 3 4 5

Notes

Get Started Hack #33
Work for Ten Minutes

Can't get started? Give yourself permission to sit down and work for only ten minutes. Set a timer. When the ten minutes are up, check in with yourself to see if you'd like to keep going. If you don't want to, stop. Walk away or try another hack. However, nine times out of ten, I'll bet you will want to keep going! Often, we simply need to stop our brain from overthinking for a few minutes in order to realize that we really are clear on what to do next.

Task or project started:

On a scale of 1–5, how did it work for you?
1 2 3 4 5

Notes

Get Started Hack #34
Listen to One Song

A great way to press pause on our brain's desire to overcomplicate things is to fill it with something different. Not sure where to start? Stop what you are doing, turn on some music, and listen to one song. Then sit down and get started on your task. After a reprieve from overthinking, you'll know how to get started!

Task or project started:

On a scale of 1–5, how did it work for you?
1   2   3   4   5

Notes

Get Started Hack #35
Do Just One

Sometimes, tasks seem *big*—too long, too much, too complicated. If you are struggling to get started when something seems like a lot, give yourself permission to do just one thing. Write just one sentence. Write just one paragraph. Read just one page. Put away just one dish. Fold just one shirt. Often, this will calm your overactive brain and after just one, you'll have clarity on how to keep going!

Task or project started:

On a scale of 1–5, how did it work for you?
1 2 3 4 5

Notes

CHAPTER 8

Mindset Hacks

We've talked about creating accountability, boosting your energy, and finding clarity. Depending on your situation, any one of these categories may offer you the hack you need to get started. But, there is one last critical category: mindset. If you've tried the others and are still struggling to get started, I encourage you to take a close look at the hacks in this chapter.

Your mindset is the way you *think* about yourself, your ability to complete a task, and your feelings around the task itself. It's the attitude with which you approach the task, and it is impacted by your personal feelings, as well as your environment.

If you think you can, you can. If you think you can't, you can't. You've probably heard this saying before, but do you believe it? It's true! Our thoughts play a huge role in whether or not we're able to get started.

Our mindset is affected by many things, but the hacks in this chapter focus on two: your belief in yourself (including your willingness to face fear and take risks) and your environment. Each of the hacks below suggests ways to boost one or the other.

Hacks #36–50

For each of the hacks in the following sections, I've included some space for you to take notes. If you try out the hack, be sure to take a moment and write down the result.

For some mindset hacks, be aware that it may take some time before you notice whether it's helpful.

Rank the hack on a scale of 1–5, with 1 meaning "it did not work at all" and 5 meaning "I started right away."

Write down the task or project you started, and, if needed, note anything that may help you to know yourself better or use this hack in the future.

Later, when you've forgotten what works and what doesn't, you'll thank yourself for those notes!

Believe in Yourself – Hacks #36–43

If you are going to start a passion project, you must believe in yourself enough to do the things that feel uncomfortable and scary. You must be willing to take risks. How much time do you spend worrying about a task? What if, instead, you simply jump in and get started? Would it save you time?

While many people would certainly prefer to have control and wait for the perfect, comfortable situation, they could be waiting a long time. You may have to stretch a bit (or a lot) as you get started on new tasks and projects. By taking small risks, you can learn to *trust yourself*, and it will be so much easier to get started (and finish)!

There are many ways to boost your belief in yourself, but most of it comes down to self-awareness. Our brains are constantly bringing up thoughts about what is going wrong in our lives, so we need to remind ourselves that plenty is going right, too! Keeping track of what's going well, having a gratitude practice, and keeping your values at the top of your mind will help you get started when the going gets rough.

Get Started Hack #36
Take a Risk

Often, we procrastinate because we are waiting for the perfect conditions. It's uncomfortable to start when we don't feel ready. If you are struggling to start, ask yourself what the worst possible outcome would be if you were to do the task despite your uncertainty. What will happen if you create the video with less-than-ideal lighting, start cleaning the closet without enough time to finish, or submit the grant with a possible typo? Stop overthinking, ditch perfectionism, and get started.

Task or project started:

On a scale of 1–5, how did it work for you?
1 2 3 4 5

Notes

Get Started Hack #37
Go for No

Sometimes "no" can be the goal. Take a risk, jump in, and expect to get a no. Write until you get a critical comment. Make calls until you have five nos. Going for no can feel quite scary. It asks you to push back on that feeling of not being ready to start. Stop worrying. After you get going, you'll likely realize it wasn't as awful as you thought it would be. It may even feel exhilarating. Everyone receives negative feedback at some point. Believe in yourself. Go for no and get started!

Task or project started:

On a scale of 1–5, how did it work for you?
1 2 3 4 5

Notes

Get Started Hack #38
Eat the Frog

This hack is the opposite of Hack #18, building momentum, and works really well for some people. It may feel uncomfortable at first, and it's not my favorite hack, but I encourage you to try eating the frog, an idea made popular by Brian Tracy. Choose your hardest, most unpleasant task and do it first. When you have checked off your most difficult item on your to-do list first thing in the morning, you'll boost your mood and feel productive for the rest of the day. Eat the frog and get started!

Task or project started:

On a scale of 1–5, how did it work for you?
1   2   3   4   5

Notes

Get Started Hack #39
Willing vs. Wanting

Some tasks are hard, and you may not want to do them, but what are you willing to do? Consider your overall intentions and goals. Believe in yourself and your ability to do hard things. When you shift your mindset from thinking about what you want (or don't want) to do and start thinking about what you are willing to do to achieve your goals, it will motivate you to get started!

Task or project started:

On a scale of 1–5, how did it work for you?
1 2 3 4 5

Notes

Get Started Hack #40
Write Affirmations

To increase your belief in yourself, it's helpful to remind yourself of what is really true. Each day we may make mistakes, have interruptions, or receive criticism, but we also make progress and positive decisions and choices. Affirmations can be powerful reminders. Popular ones include, "Anything is possible," "I am building my future," and, "I believe in my dreams, myself, and all that I am." Choose statements that feel best and write them down repeatedly, each day.

Task or project started:

On a scale of 1–5, how did it work for you?
1 2 3 4 5

Notes

Get Started Hack #41
Think About Your Values

When you're feeling stuck, it's often helpful to remember your values. Consider why you wanted to work toward your dream in the first place. Are you a helpful person? Generous? Compassionate? Are you a leader? A team player? Are you striving to make the world a better place? What do you value in others and what can you do today to exhibit this value in your own life? Remembering what you value can give you a boost to get started!

Task or project started:

On a scale of 1–5, how did it work for you?
1 2 3 4 5

Notes

Get Started Hack #42
Be Grateful

We have so much to be grateful for, if we only slow down enough to notice. Start a gratitude practice by writing down a few things you are grateful for each day. Notice the people in your life (both those you know and those you haven't actually met), the things that make your life easier, and the opportunities that make you a better person. As you consider what you are grateful for each day, you will begin to notice more and more. Being grateful will boost your mood and help you get started!

Task or project started:

On a scale of 1–5, how did it work for you?
1   2   3   4   5

Notes

Get Started Hack #43
Create an Evidence List

Something is always going well in your life. Your brain would like to tell you otherwise, but I promise there is always something to celebrate. Write down the small wins or progress you make each week. Even if all you did was make one phone call, it is evidence of moving toward your goal. Most weeks, you'll have plenty more to add to your list. When you are frustrated and unmotivated, review your evidence list as proof that you are making progress. This will provide the motivation to get started!

Task or project started:

Notes

On a scale of 1–5, how did it work for you?
1 2 3 4 5

Adjust Your Environment – Hacks #44–50

In addition to the feelings about ourselves and about the task itself, our environment also affects our mindset. The space we live and work in, as well as the people around us, impact our mood and our ability to get started.

A few years ago, I attended a workshop where they talked about tiny little changes you can make to adjust your environment and boost your motivation. Choosing a different pen could be the difference between procrastination or checking an item off your to-do list. I've explored this idea ever since and helped many clients make tiny, simple changes that have had huge impacts on their moods and propelled them into action. Sight, sound, scent, touch, taste—all five senses offer different opportunities to jump-start your motivation.

Look around. What do you see? How does it make you feel? Does your environment motivate you or drain you? Don't underestimate the power your surroundings have on your productivity! The people, colors, objects, sounds, and more have a great impact on our moods and mindsets. In turn, we feel excited, motivated, and happy, or we feel anxious, unmotivated, and sad.

Take this idea a step further. In addition to looking at the stuff around you, who surrounds you? Think about your family and friends. Are they positive or negative people? Do they lift you up or drag you down? Do you watch and listen to inspirational, upbeat, successful people?

Sometimes, when I watch a bit too much TV or spend too much time scrolling through social media, I feel drained. I'm merely sitting there "resting," but I don't feel rested! In contrast, I can spend a whole day on my feet talking to a group of entrepreneurial women and walk away feeling energized.

Get Started Hack #44
Look Around

Take a look around. What do you see? Who do you see? Your environment can have a huge impact on your productivity. Choose colors, images, and objects that bring you joy. Surround yourself with people who lift you up and encourage you. You will feel a boost of motivation with each small change. As you remove negativity and add positivity, your whole life will begin to shift. Look around, surround yourself with joy, and get started!

Task or project started:

On a scale of 1–5, how did it work for you?
1 2 3 4 5

Notes

Get Started Hack #45
Listen to Inspiration

If you want positive energy, borrow some from someone else! We have music, podcasts, videos, and audiobooks at our fingertips every day. Choose your favorite motivational speaker, listen to an upbeat song, or watch an inspiring story. Then get started!

Task or project started:

On a scale of 1–5, how did it work for you?
1   2   3   4   5

Notes

Get Started Hack #46
Choose a Scent

We often overlook the power of scent! They say that baking cookies prior to an open house encourages buyers to purchase a home. People buy flowers to add a fresh fragrance to their day. Essential oil diffusers, air fresheners, and scented candles bring aromas into your personal space. What scents do you love? Something uplifting to motivate you or something soothing to slow you down? Find one you love and use it while working on a specific task or project.

Task or project started:

On a scale of 1–5, how did it work for you?
1 2 3 4 5

Notes

Get Started Hack #47
Listen to Music

Some people thrive in quiet environments and may prefer silence. They become distracted by people talking, music playing, or even birds or cars passing by. Others need sound! They find they can focus better with some background noise. If you prefer to have sound, try turning on some music to set the mood you want. Choose the artist, genre, volume, and rhythm that motivates you. You can even create a playlist for specific tasks—upbeat songs for cleaning the house or low-key music for studying.

Task or project started:

On a scale of 1–5, how did it work for you?
1 2 3 4 5

Notes

Get Started Hack #48
Select a New Pen

Do you love office supplies? Pretty paper, new journals, and fancy pens can all be quite motivating! Different pens and paper types offer a new feel, something different to touch and hold. If you have a project that seems daunting, try using a special pen (or highlighter, pencil, marker, etc.). Select a fun shape, style, or color only for this occasion, something you will look forward to using. Take out your new pen and get started!

Task or project started:

On a scale of 1–5, how did it work for you?
1 2 3 4 5

Notes

Get Started Hack #49
Adjust the Lights

After many years of working in classrooms, I realized the fluorescent overhead lighting drained me and caused headaches. As a result, I filled my classroom with lamps with regular light bulbs. In my home, I open the curtains to let in the sunlight. If you are struggling to get started, check your lighting. Do you need more or less? Do you need different light bulbs? Do you need to sit near a window? You can even try different colored light bulbs for a fun change. Adjust the lighting and get started!

Task or project started:

On a scale of 1–5, how did it work for you?
1 2 3 4 5

Notes

Get Started Hack #50
Clean Your Space

I love a clean desk. Sometimes, especially before harder tasks, I will clean up my office. Papers are sorted and filed, everything is put back in its home, and a clear work surface becomes ready. I never understood this behavior until I began observing more about my own motivation. You see, when my desk is cluttered, my brain is cluttered, and when my brain is cluttered, I procrastinate. Clean your space and get started!

Task or project started:

On a scale of 1–5, how did it work for you?
1 2 3 4 5

Notes

CHAPTER 9
You've Reached the End!

Whether you've tried all 50 hacks or only a few, I sincerely hope you've learned a bit about yourself along the way. If you've finished your project or have a long way to go, I hope you have identified a few strategies to get restarted again and again.

Getting started is not the end-all-be-all of success. It is merely one piece of the puzzle. There are not always quick solutions for handling our feelings of overwhelm, learning to avoid distractions, planning ahead, and staying focused. If there were, we'd all be superstars. However, I do believe implementing these hacks is the first step.

Whatever your passion project is, it's likely you are both excited and hesitant at the same time. I've felt the same way during the two years I've worked on this book! You lead a busy life, there are many distractions, and your project likely feels overwhelming. All of this is true, yet it is also true that it's time to kick these excuses to the curb. It is possible to keep making progress if you stay connected to your passion, do what works for you (not others), and keep getting started (or restarted).

My mission is to offer you some guidance on how to get started on your goals, even if you put the "pro" in procrastination. I believe you can get started and restarted, even if you have learning and attention issues that have held you back in the past. I haven't outlined a prescription for success; instead, I've offered 50 options from which you can choose because I know every brain is unique, and you need to figure out what works best for you.

You are creative, talented, and ambitious! You have an amazing idea, a dream, a passion the world is waiting for. Don't let procrastination get in the way. If you've worked your way through this book and continue to struggle with getting started, I encourage you to go back and read the first few chapters. You may need to reconnect with your passion, revisit why you're struggling to get started, or learn a bit more about yourself before choosing and finding the hacks that work.

If, after that, you're still looking for additional support, please connect with me using one of the options below:

- For daily tips and encouragement, follow my Facebook page @barbhubbardcoaching.

- For a supportive community of women who can offer accountability, time management tips, and encouragement, check out my virtual member community, How to Eat an Elephant: A Community for Busy Women (https://barbhubbardcoaching.com/how-to-eat-an-elephant/).

- For one-on-one guidance to figure out what will work best for you, I'd love to have a free discovery call with you to explore coaching (https://calendly.com/barbhubbard/discovery-session).

I want to hear about your dreams, your goals, your passion projects, and how you are making an impact on the world! Which hacks helped you get started? Email me at barb@barbhubbardcoaching.com and let me know!

Whether you end up becoming a hack master or need a helping hand along the way, keep going! The world needs your passion!

Cheering you on,

50 Getting Started Hacks

1. Go to a Virtual Work Session
2. Collaborate with a Partner
3. Hire Support People
4. Schedule First
5. Ask for a Deadline
6. Reward Yourself
7. Sprint
8. Share First
9. Switch Seats
10. Change Your Scenery
11. Go for a Walk

12. Do Jumping Jacks
13. Move While Working
14. Gather Your Supplies
15. Dance
16. Have Fun First
17. Be Generous
18. Build Momentum
19. Work at a Different Time of Day
20. Tap Into Your Creative Side
21. Plan a Strategic Work Hour
22. Eat a Healthy Snack
23. Go to Sleep
24. Take a Nap
25. Meditate
26. Take a Breath
27. Draw It
28. Make a List
29. Write It Out
30. Visualize
31. Talk About It
32. Know Your "Why"

33. Work for Ten Minutes
34. Listen to One Song
35. Do Just One
36. Take a Risk
37. Go for No
38. Eat the Frog
39. Willing vs. Wanting
40. Write Affirmations
41. Think About Your Values
42. Be Grateful
43. Create an Evidence List
44. Look Around
45. Listen to Inspiration
46. Choose a Scent
47. Listen to Music
48. Select a New Pen
49. Adjust the Lights
50. Clean Your Space

Acknowledgements

This book is the result of a lifetime of trying to figure out how to get started. It would not have been possible without the support and guidance of many amazing people.

First and foremost, I must acknowledge my loving husband Robert and my amazing children, Christopher and Sydney. Your love, encouragement, and support has meant the world to me. I love you more than words can express. The unwavering belief you have in me is the reason this book is now out in the world. A special shout-out to Sydney who designed the cover and assisted with editing. Your creativity blows me away.

This book would not be possible without the guidance of book coach extraordinaire Danielle Anderson. You pulled ideas and content out of me that I didn't know was there. And you provided the accountability I needed to restart, over and over.

Thank you to my clients. Each and every one of you has offered an original perspective into this topic. I am fascinated by your unique brains, I love your passion, and I have been honored to walk alongside you for part of your journey.

I am also blessed to know two truly amazing humans who have believed in me when I didn't believe in myself. Ruth Loh and Judy Corasaniti, you each entered my life at exactly the right moment. Ruth, thank you for teaching me to own my power and approach life with grace and ease. Judy, your encouragement means the world to me.

A few years ago, I took a leap of faith and joined a women's connection group. I was scared beyond belief and my confidence was non-existent. To each and every woman I have met through Polka Dot Powerhouse, thank you—your support has been a game changer. I have learned so much from you and have grown by leaps and bounds. Sara Torpey, you sit on my shoulder and encourage me every day. Patricia White, thank you for the edits and feedback on this book. Rachael Davila, I would not want to be on this journey without you. LeAnn Erimli, your technical abilities astound me. And to all the women in Southern California, both past and present members, you hold a special place in my heart.

Finally, thank you readers! I believe we are all on a journey of self-discovery. As you figure out how to start and restart, I'm excited to see where your passions take you.

About the Author

Barb Hubbard is a Time Management Coach and ADHD Specialist. She loves supporting ambitious individuals who have BIG GOALS! She sees the strengths and endless possibility in others and lovingly guides them to discover it in themselves. With compassion and understanding, she helps her clients move forward with their vision by breaking it into organized and manageable steps and guiding them to the finish line. Barb expertly helps big dreamers discover clarity, find their focus, and feel motivated to work on the big and scary projects on their to-do list!

Barb started her career as an elementary-level special education teacher. After many years of teaching children and supporting parents, Barb began to notice that distractibility, forgetfulness, and disorganization weren't limited to the classroom. Adults were asking for support after discovering that they too were living with ADHD. Even friends shared that they were finding it increasingly difficult to start and grow their businesses in our fast-paced, distracting society. So, in 2018, Barb launched her coaching business.

Barb's special talent is looking at a huge project or task and knowing how to break it down into small attainable steps, prioritizing what to work on first, and acting as a trusted accountability partner to help people see projects through to the end. She is well-versed in the challenges of time management, organization, and productivity. Barb's motto is, "Find peace in the chaos; be productive, not just busy!"

Made in United States
Troutdale, OR
09/16/2025